Faith &

Spirituality

A QUANTUM MOMENT OF **DISCOVERY AND PURPOSE**

Andre Pierce MDiv. C.P.E.

Printed in the United States of America.

Cover Design by 100Covers.com
Interior Design by FormattedBooks.com

Dedication

This book is dedicated to those human souls recorded throughout the world who have had a profound spiritual experience which change their lives and put their life's journey on a new course and destiny. It is a book designed to encourage those who struggle with sharing their spiritual experience with people who don't believe in one's life having purpose and life after death.

PRELUDE

In this period of spiritual discovery, I found some interesting thoughts about my religious beliefs and how spirituality affected its conclusions. My traditional religious background and history brought me through life's test and challenges. However, I didn't know the depth of how spiritual I was until I completed my studies in clinical pastoral education while interviewing a few people who had been to the other side of life and came back to talk about what they experienced. That exposure brought me to a richer and more rewarding level of spirituality than I had ever known before. The experience gave me a clearer understanding of what drives a purpose-driven life. My hope is that this book will bring about the same spiritual awareness, curiosity, and enlightenment that it brought me. I pray that your religion, no matter what faith you have chosen, will be greatly enriched by spiritual knowledge and understanding that nothing in the universe dies; it's transformed.

CHAPTER 1

I'm a son of a Baptist pastor who converted to Methodist and the grandson of a Baptist pastor, which gave me some form of religious origin and instilled in me some kind of moral code of ethics. I liked living up to that moral code or not. Being the pastor's son was like living in a fishbowl, not easy. The family on my mother's side were Methodist and not too particularly committed to their faith. In fact, most of them went to church when it was convenient. They occasionally talked about Jesus but had no personal relationship with him. However, my mother and grandmother were committed to the church. On the other hand, the family on my father's side, which was a very large family of Baptist folks, were extremely religious. Aunts, uncles, cousins, dogs, cats, and farm animals were all committed to the church and God. I believed that I was Baptist born and Baptist bred, and that when I die, I'll be Baptist dead. Although I went to church and participated by singing in the choir or ushering people in, I still felt like a rebel without a cause. I had a spirit looking for excitement, not knowing that it was a sense of purpose I was searching for. At that time, I hadn't bought into the church thing. At The age of nineteen, I found a sense of belonging with a band that traveled around the country, playing gigs here and there. I was only allowed to do this if it didn't interfere with church attendance on Sunday. My parents allowed me to mind my own business until I found myself. You know how it is when clubbing is more important and exciting than church. When praying and reading the Bible is replaced by satisfying my own ego. This is the kind of life that most of us get caught up in while fulfilling our egos. Minding my own business means focusing on what was important to me, getting my needs met, for example, buying a car, making money, having a sense of adventure, working, having many girlfriends, etc. The more I got, the more I wanted. The church wasn't a top priority or focus because it didn't provide that kind of excitement. Even with that understanding, I felt a small but persistent pull on my heart to a greater purpose. I wasn't aware of nor did I believe that God was still in control. I always knew God existed because I was taught that. I remember somewhere in the Bible where it reads, "Train a child in the path they should go and they will not depart from it." My family took that responsibility very serious. There was no place in our family for atheists or agnostics to find solace. I learned that when you follow the ego of self-fulfillment there's no place for God or any form of a higher power. Interestingly, I could hide the traits of my ego while attending church.

Between the ages of 19 and 23, I worked at a state hospital as an orderly serving mentally ill patients. My mother got me that job because she wanted me to work and not stay home doing nothing. Also, it would keep me out of my father's wrath. My father believed that if a man doesn't work, you ought to break his plate. Although I worked there, I didn't see it as serving others. I was in my ego, once again unaware that God was in control. I still played in the rock band, hoping to be discovered as a rock star while still working at the state hospital. At that time, the Vietnam war was going on, and I was concerned that my number would come up for the draft, so I enrolled into college. It was understood at that time that if you were in college, you could avoid the draft. Although I only completed two classes in a junior college, I never got drafted. I was driven by the fear of the draft and Vietnam because a lot of my friends who went never came back. I had no evidence that I was going to be drafted nor was it real because I had no draft card; I only had the possibility. So, I learned that the word "fear" means False Evidence Appearing Real. Fear is a thought, which is mental and can manufacture anxiety, causing panic attacks and worry. You cannot see a thought because it's mental, which drives you to act out that thought by fleeing. It's like an invisible virus that finds its way in the vortex of your mind. Once you focus on it, it dictates your reality. Fear can decapitate you and cause you to flee instead of confront. Fear, like all emotions, is by choice. You don't have to be afraid; you choose to be. There are always some external stimuli that provoke you to make an emotional decision and response. Because fear is a mental thing, it will drive you to nightmares, anxiety attacks, high blood pressures, and isolation. What you confront is real, but fear isn't an option to confront things that are real. When you don't focus on fear, you can walk through chaos cool, calm, and collected. One thing that can get you through troubled times, worry, and even grief is to focus on your purpose. We often fail because we haven't recognized our purpose, what the Creator designed you to do with your life. When you focus on fulfilling your purpose, you can face obstacles; you don't notice the chaos around you. I call that walking on water. God hasn't given you the spirit of fear but of a sound mind. Thus, fear is a choice of the will. Once you concur by choosing not to be fearful, you can live in confidence that no weapon formed against you shall prosper. The effect of your reality is only as real as you choose it to be.

As I worked at the state hospital, I was offered a scholarship to an LPN. nursing school. While there, I met my first girlfriend. I wondered why I never completed the program after that. Once again, I was minding my own business and fulfilling my ego. I was still in the rock band where all kinds of girls would throw themselves at me, so, obviously, my ego was being filled. I was still attending church; I had to, living in my father's house. Although my father was the pastor of the church, he also was a POW. And suffered from the effects of post-traumatic stress disorder (PTSD). So, as long as I was in his house, I didn't question if I was going to church without receiving an immediate response verbally or physically. I was fearful of him, so, as a youth, although I was around it a lot, I never experienced drugs or drinking for fear he would find out. During those years, I began to feel the need to move out of his house.

On Christmas day 1971, my sister died of an aneurism at the age of eighteen. I remember a pastoral friend of my father came by and prayed for her while she was in a coma on a respirator in intensive care. During his prayer my sisters color seem to return giving hope that she was coming out it. A few minutes later, she flatlined. When that happened, I found it interesting that I never questioned God's ability to bring her back to life. I had more faith and hope in the power of the pastor's prayer than I did in God's ability to heal her. I didn't know then what I know now that my sister was having a profound experience in the near-death zone between heaven and Earth. It is a time when a decision has to be made to reenter one's body or transition to the other side. She made her choice.

At the age of twenty-five I left home and the band to see what it was like to be on my own. Leaving the band was the most difficult thing I had ever done. I was leaving friends and the possibility of being discovered in the music industry. So, I moved in with a cousin of mine in Jacksonville, Florida. Since I had a history of working in a hospital, I was able to get a part time job working at a local clinic for troubled youth. During my stay with my cousin, she began pressuring me to take responsibility and pull my load or get out. I was biding my time, delaying the process of entering school again for nursing. By this time, I hated school and thought it just wasn't for me. I was just trying to prolong the inevitable. My cousin kicked me out; I was homeless. But I still had a part-time job and lived in my car. I ate cinnamon buns and milk daily. This went on for about eight months. I wasn't attending any church at all because I was now minding my own business, once again unaware that God was moving in my life. I was still not aware of the hostile takeover that was coming.

After an eight-month period of homelessness, I was depressed and decided to call my father and ask him if I could come home to live with him. When he said yes, I felt the depression leaving and hope restored. I'm reminded of the biblical passage about the prodigal son in Luke 15:11-32. I had left home but was finally returning. I was trying to find my way home through minding my own business and doing my own thing, which, apparently, wasn't working. It seems that God gives us enough rope for us to hang ourselves and uses that same rope to pull us to him. I had no idea at the time that he was setting me up for a hostile takeover.

Once I returned home, living in my father's house, church was mandatory; no debate there. I was twenty-six now and starting to become frustrated with the church, but I couldn't leave. After attending church for about two months, my father asked me to attend one of his Bible studies that he was having at the church. I didn't feel comfortable about that, so I always had something else to do. When he left for the study group, something within me said, "You should have gone." The next week he asked the same question and like usual I refused. Interestingly, my father never forced the issue; perhaps he was changing to. Several weeks went by with the same question asked, same answer given, and each week, the same voice said to me, "You should have gone." This voice became stronger each week to the point I thought someone audibly saying to me, "You should have gone." This inward pull became relentless to the point that it scared me. I thought I was schizophrenic and losing my mind by hearing voices. I asked myself, "Why is this happening? I never had a strong feeling like this before." If I did, I didn't recognize it, so now I'm scared to go to the church. So, I prayed for the first time in my life to God, "If you are real, as if I didn't know it, prove it to me where I can understand. Amen!" That was it. I didn't think about it anymore. I just went about my life minding my own business and doing my own thing. You know, one thing I've learned is that God has a way of showing up when you aren't looking for it, particularly when you're minding your own business. There comes a time in your life when you let go of your defense mechanism and unwittingly receive suggestion by a higher power. When that happens, I call that your opportunity for a quantum moment. The beginning of my quantum moment was taking place. It was about several months after that prayer out of anger that he showed up. It was a Saturday night. I felt good inside. And as the night went on, I was feeling better and better. The best way to describe it was I felt like a child on Christmas eve finding it difficult to sleep the night before. I thought I have no place to go the next day but to church, so why am I so excited. I wasn't aware that this was the early stages of the hostile takeover. The feeling was so intense it lasted until six o'clock Sunday morning. At that time, I made up my mind that I wasn't going to church because I was up all night with a feeling I can only describe as overjoyous, and that description is very inadequate. At that time, I fell asleep. I woke up about an hour later and felt like I had slept all night and was well rested. And yes, I was still feeling overjoyous. I decided to go to church, but it was different this time, for I found myself having great difficulty staying seated. This overjoyous feeling was so intense, I had to get up and hug everybody. I know they thought something was wrong with me, but they only smiled back. It seems that they knew a secret that I didn't know. We had a visiting minster that day and I don't remember anything he preached because I was emotionally detached and caught up in this overjoyous feeling of euphoria and I was about to explode. I remember the prophet Jeremiah 20:9 saying that "his word was in my heart as a burning fire shut up in my bones." I was having a profound spiritual experience. On the way home after the worship service, I started crying. I couldn't understand this, since I was feeling so good. I couldn't wait to get home and tell my father how I was feeling. I immediately pulled him into his bedroom, and before I could ask him, different languages were coming out of my mouth. My father looked surprised and happy at the same time. He knew what was happening to me. I guess the secret was out; he told me that I had experienced the baptism of the Holy Spirit. It was a hostile takeover, resulting in a mental paradigm shift. It was God's way of answering a prayer I ask several months before and forgot about. I discovered that this experience interfered with me minding my own business. I called this a hostile takeover because while minding my own business, I was interrupted by a quantum moment. Some may call it the baptism of the Holy Spirit, some may call it a mental and spiritual paradigm shift, and some may even call the experience an awakening or salvation. All labels seem to be appropriate. I choose to call it a quantum event or moment where I experienced a shift in my spirit of thinking and interest.

Four things happen when this event comes: (1) it's vivid, giving you a sense of clarity; (2) it's a surprise, so you don't see it coming; (3) it's benevolent with overjoyous/good feelings coming with it; and (4) it's enduring, lasting forever. You can never forget because it totally changes the way you think. Although my quantum moment happened over 40 years ago, it still feels like it just happened. At that time, I had a strong urge or pull to get to know God more, so I became ridiculously hungry for the Word of God and began reading books by people who had the same experience that

I had so I could compare notes. I began reading a lot of religious materials to the point where I only slept about three hours a night yet I still felt rested. This went on for about three months.

One thing I would like to interject here that resulted from my quantum moment was a change in the relationship I had with my girlfriend at the time. Before the quantum moment, we were in torment regularly every night. After my quantum moment, she noticed a clear change in me. So, she told me that she had to reevaluate our relationship. WHAT! She meant that we were no longer having sex because I was saved now, and that form of our relationship was now inappropriate. Hearing that hurt a lot. I felt my heart breaking; I felt our relationship was over because I got saved. Depression set in, and I began to think that this salvation, this new way of thinking, this spiritual paradigm shift, this quantum moment came at the inappropriate time. After about a week of hurting and a lot of crying, I sat on the side of the bed and began to pray out loud, "Lord, I need you to help me get over this heartbreak, please." As I was ending my prayer, I felt the pressure on the bed as though someone had sat down beside me. I became scared because no one was in the room but me. I was afraid to look behind me to see who was on the bed. After about five minutes, the pressure on the bed disappeared, and I immediately felt my depression and heartbreak leave me. I felt joy, the same overjoyous feeling I had during my quantum moment. I turn around to see who was on the bed, but nobody was there. I knew then that God's presence was in that room comforting me because I asked. More evidence for me that he is real. Also, I began to feel sorry for my girlfriend who wasn't saved or didn't experience a quantum moment like I had. She wasn't interested because, at that point, I was forcing my religion on her, making her very uncomfortable to be around me, so she eventually moved out. I guess I was a holy roller; I wanted everybody to experience what I went through.

Other things that changed in me was the use of profanity. The words came in my thoughts, but I was unable to speak them. That was a WOW revelation for me. I started replacing those words with "all, shoot, dog gone it, I'll be john brown." I realized that I wasn't stopping my profanity; I was now practicing sin management. Although the words were replaced; the emotional energy was still driving it. And that's what God wanted me to look at and address. I was just on the front porch with my heart getting clean up. I needed to go into the house where the real work begins. I needed to prepare myself for the work that God wanted me to do.

I felt a strong urge to attend a seminary to further my curiosity and to satisfy this newfound religious appetite. I had attended college before and failed, but I believed that this inward pulling, for some reason, wouldn't let me fail. At twenty-six, I began shadowing my father in the church and became an associate minister of the church. I was indeed a changed man, a new person. Hell, I didn't recognize myself, but I was confident that that was what I was supposed to do at that time. Collage grants and student loans became available to me, which was a surprise. I then was told that I had to have a B.A. degree first to enroll in the seminary because it was a graduate program. I became a little disappointed because I thought attending an undergraduate school would be a distraction. But I accepted that I had to go through that process, so I enrolled in Virginia Union University and majored in urban studies. Living on campus was a little difficult because most of the students there were between eighteen and twenty-one. I was twenty-seven and one of the older men on campus, so the school made me the dorm director. That was unexpected, but God was in control, and I needed a paycheck. That position afforded me the opportunity to council and guide the younger students through their life issues. I was again honing my counseling skills while serving others. While in undergraduate school, I was called to a church that needed a pastor in the local area. I may have bitten off more than I could chew pastoring full time and being a full-time student. But somehow or other, God got me through that. Once I graduated from the undergraduate studies, I was glad to get to the main course, the seminary. I was happy my first year there until they took my Jesus away. One of the ways this was done was through a course of study called "the plunge." This course of study was designed for you to experience what would it be like to be on the streets where you had to survive with just $2.50 for two weeks. Rules where you couldn't have any

I.D. other than your social security card, no watches, and no wallet. The police knew we were out there, and we were only to contact them in case of an emergency, which, for me, just being out there was an emergency. What was more interesting about this course was that it was only offered in January and you had to choose from three cities to experience your study: Baltimore, New York, or Chicago. I chose Baltimore. The day my plunge was to begin, it was cold and raining, and the moment I was put off that bus to experience homelessness, I felt depressed. So, I immediately understood how homeless people feel. The only difference for me was that in two weeks, I knew it was going to be over. Being on that street, I felt that God had left me. I had to find shelter and food, which was a challenge because at the first McDonald's I came across, I spent my $2.50. I looked at my schedule a noticed that I had thirteen more days to go. One thing I learned following my experience was that the only way I could understand hard times was to experience what it was like to go without. I began to preach from a different perspective now. One experience I had while on the street was visiting strip clubs just to stay warm. Although I saw more than I wanted to see, you had to buy a drink to stay before they ran you out. I had to do whatever it took to stay warm; it was 2 degrees outside at the time. From that experience, I also found out that you could stay in hospital waiting rooms for several hours before they asked if you were there waiting for someone. If not, they would ask you to leave. Also, you can stay at a bus station for several hours before the police run you out. What a learning experience. I went to a church on a Bible study night and asked one of the leaders of the church if he could direct me or tell me where I could get a bowl of soup. This leader cursed me out with a Bible under his arm and told me that he was going to have me locked up for loitering if I didn't leave the church grounds. WOW! When that course was over, I went to the pastor of that church and told him about the experience I had with one of his members. The pastor told me that he wouldn't apologize for his member's behaviors. He said the this is often the reality of the church. Don't believe in any illusions that because you're the pastor, your members will listen to what you preach. You can preach and teach how to love your neighbor as yourself, but some folks suffer from selective hearing and choose not to act on what they know is the right thing to do, especially when they're out of sight of the pastor. At that point, I felt that God had left me and I was in the wilderness. Did God really call me to do this ministry, particularly when folks don't listen? I assumed that people will make the decision to obey the will of God, even with having a quantum moment. I began to question my calling for two years until they gave my Jesus back to me in my third year. I was a Holy Roller before seminary, but afterwards, my theology became sound and focused. I learned from the experience of taking my Jesus away that if you're too heavenly minded you can do no one any earthly good. Seminary brought me down to earth. Upon graduation from the seminary, I still had a persistent and consistent inward pulling to a more challenging ministry of purpose.

CHAPTER 2

A fellow seminarian of mine who graduated a year ahead of me came back to the seminary wearing a naval officer's uniform. He was there to recruit those who were interested in military chaplaincy. This was Interesting to me because it was the same time the movie, *An Officer and a Gentleman* came out. I was feeling the need to join the military as a navy chaplain, so I resign my pastorate and went active duty. I remember thinking to myself that if I were to join the military it should be the navy or air force because my father was in the army, and I didn't want to be in harm's way. You know, sleeping in the woods on the ground while bullets are flying around; that's what I call, in harm's way. So, the navy decision came easy. However, the navy stationed me with the marine corps where I was in harm's way sleeping in the woods with a pack on my back. When I told my father about where I was stationed, he said to me that I got exactly what I deserved. I never was stationed on a ship the whole time I was in the navy. However, despite this, life appeared to be moving normally for me. I looked back over my life and thought God had brought me a long way. I believed that now I was following God's plan for me. My faith was strong as a Baptist minister and former pastor, and things were going well until I was informed that if you were performing institutional ministry for the government like a veteran's hospital or military, you aren't permitted to prophesize or try to convert someone to your faith group. That was frustrating, unless the person was asking for it; then they were free game. You can preach and teach them but no forced conversion. This is what they meant by the separation of church and state. Even though I was uncomfortable with this, I settle in with the idea. After four years of military service, I was able to continue my ministry in the VA hospital. While an employee of the VA hospital, I was offered the opportunity to enroll in a course of study called Clinical Pastoral Education (C.P.E.). This course of study is designed to help you address any emotional or mental issues that you've been struggling with. The reason for this is that if you haven't addressed those issues within yourself, you aren't qualified to help anyone else. So, in other words, if you had a hole in your soul, C.P.E. would find it. I had now become one of God's wounded healers. Since I was now working as part of the clinical team, I needed to be qualified to be on that team of psychiatrist, phycologist, clinical social workers, clinical nurse specialist, clinical chaplain, and a counselor. At first, it was difficult for me when, after an interview with a veteran patient, I was asked of my assessment by the lead psychiatrist. I tried to be as clinical as possible in my response. For an example, I would say, "the patient seems to be struggling with a dual personality." When the psychiatrist heard that, he stopped me and said, "Can't you see that this patient is demonic?" If I wanted the answer you gave, I would have asked the members of the clinical team. I'm looking for a spiritual assessment not a clinical assessment. That's why you're on the team." Well, that freed me up and taught me to stay in my lane and to make a sound spiritual assessment. At that time, I was exposed to veterans who had experienced NDEs (near-death experiences). Even though I was a religious man and believed in the hereafter, I never imagine someone dying and coming back to tell anyone. Jesus said in John 14:3 "I will go and prepare a place for you that where I am you may be also." I just didn't believe that it was possible to see heaven and come back and tell about it. So, I began my research; I wanted to learn more about this near-death phenomenon.

First, I started interviewing veterans in hospice units and particularly those who had to be revived in the O.R. but were now waiting for the conclusion of their lives. Some said that during their resuscitation, they saw relatives who died and came to greet them. To them, the experience was more vivid than a dream. They told me that they were afraid to tell anyone because no one would believe them. One veteran said that when he told his doctor, the doctor put him on some medication to address hallucinations or put him on the psych ward for some evaluation or observation. So that patient kept his mouth shut and didn't tell anybody he didn't trust. It was refreshing for him to be able to tell me, someone he trusted who believed that he wasn't hallucinating but was experiencing something profound.

It has been known throughout the medical communities that when your brain loses oxygen, you begin to hallucinate. Thus, these visions are considered to be the results of an oxygen-starved brain. This common understanding was shared by Dr. Eben Alexander a neurosurgeon until he had an NDE. Dr. Alexander was in a comma while his brain was being attacked by bacterial meningitis, which made it impossible for his brain to experience any hallucinations or visions. He wrote that before his NDE he believed very little about NDE because it didn't fit the model of a dying brain. However, many of the typical elements of the NDE were part of his experience beyond death. In his book, *Proof of Heaven*, he describes a deep sense of peace, a portal into another world, the all-encompassing knowledge, and the presence of pure love manifested by this beautiful girl sitting on a butterfly wing. He claims he was in a heavenly place riding on the wings of a butterfly with a beautiful girl he had never seen before who was telling him that he could do no wrong there, that everything was well, and that he was loved and cherished there. Months later, the meaningful appearance of this beautiful girl, whom he hadn't met in real life, gave him confirmation of the reality of his experience. Dr. Alexander was given into adoption when he was two weeks old. About a year before his comma, he finally visited his birth parents for the first time and met his biological sister and brother. A younger sister, Betsy, had sadly died some years earlier. A few months after his comma, when his birth parents sent him a picture of Betsy, he realized that the beautiful girl on the butterfly wing was his younger sister who had passed away. He further explained that our materialistic worldview leads us away from the fact that we are divine beings, pure consciousness, and eternal spiritual entities. Dr. Alexander wrote that all the medical training he had from Harvard and the science he taught couldn't explain his experience. Bacterial meningitis leaves no room for a near-death experience, yet he came back with a rich odyssey fresh in his mind. The reductive materialistic science disappeared in his mind. A supernatural world exists all around us that's more real than our reality. Dr. Alexander concluded what he learned was that "where medicine ends, true life begins."

Dr. Mary Neal, a spinal cord specialist was on a kayaking trip in South America. During the trip, her kayak turned over and she was under eight feet of water at the base of a waterfall without oxygen for 30 minutes before CPR could be administered. When she regained consciousness, she was in a state of shock, not because she had drowned, not because her legs were broken, and not because she was in a very remote location away from any immediate care. She was shocked because she couldn't believe that she was sent back from a place she could only describe as heaven. It was peaceful under water. She was held and comforted by spiritual beings. She was taken through a life review that had little to do with judgment but everything to do with understanding, compassion, and grace. She stated that she was shown the beauty that came out of every heartbreak, every challenge, and every disappointment of her life. And then she was greeted by spiritual beings who had loved her since the beginning of time, beings she had known since forever. Even as she was observing the beautiful colors and smells of heaven, she was able to look back at her blotted purple body as her husband and friends started CPR. She recognized her body and she knew she was dead, but, despite having a wonderful life with a successful career and beautiful children and husband whom she loved more that life itself, she felt like she was home and had no intention of returning or going back to that life. Then she was told that it wasn't her time, that she had more work to do. When she objected, she was given a laundry list of things she needed to do. What was interesting to me about her story was that she was raised in the church, but she had left that belief and followed the scientific and medical path. She was confident, smart, intellectual, and started to believe that she didn't need God. She was now a mixture of humanist, materialist, scientific rationalist, and maybe a cultural Christian. She said that the underwater experience seemed real, but God was the only reality, which started her journey of spiritual enlightenment. She spent many months in her hospital in bed trying to make sense of what happen to her. She searched for scientific answers and looked at her medical records with the people who had been with her at the river with the strong desire to forget everything she had been told. She then read extensively about drowning, psychology of the dying brain, hallucinations, and neurotransmitter dumping. But all those conventional theories fell short of explaining what happen to her, and nothing could account for her spiritual experience. Over 20 million people in this country alone have had a neardeath experience.

Every breath we share is a divine miracle; every experience is a miracle. The reality of earthly things we take for granted are miracles that we often don't even notice.

I watched the movie *The Forgiven*, directed by Clint Eastwood. The main character had near-death experience that was horrifying. When he was revived, he stated that he now noticed the trees and the mountains that he didn't notice before.

Many people who had near-death experiences have often stated that when they were there in that heavenly place, they didn't want to come back. Some became angry at their doctors for providing resuscitation procedures to bring them back. They wanted to stay because it was home for them. One lady said that she found herself arguing with Jesus when he told her she had to go back because her work wasn't done. These people no longer fear death. Once they've been on the other side, they now look forward for their life's end with joy and confident. They don't want to end it prematurely, but they were no longer fearful of the transition. However, some had to be put on suicide watch because they no longer feared death and wanted to return right away. One veteran shared with me the NDE he had while on the battlefield. He said that after he was shot, he felt no pain after the first bullet hit him, what was odd and strange for him was that he could see more bullets coming at him in slow motion, hitting his body but he felt no pain only joy. The veteran knew he was dead because he was standing in his spirit by the medic who was trying to revive him. What a profound experience we as humans are going to go through during our transition to the afterlife. Whether you believe it or not, it's going to happen, and there's nothing you can do about it. Every human being is going to experience this phenomenon, no one can escape this experience.

One thing I have learned from these veterans about death is that "**NO ONE DIES ALONE!**" It doesn't matter if you're homeless, have no family, or are away from family members. "**NO ONE DIES ALONE!**" Upon your death, spiritual beings are there to greet you and assist you in your transition. Sometimes, it's a family member or friend who passed away years before your death, but someone in the spiritual world is always there to assist you in your transition. What will happen is:

1. you'll receive an unconditional loving welcome
2. you'll still be you, but a deeper you
3. you'll be free to go where ever you want
4. you'll have a life review
5. you'll have opportunities to learn and progress

When we die, we'll be chaperoned by angelic beings who are conduits of God's love for you. You'll establish a very close connection with these angels. They'll guard against any negativity that's inside of you. Many people who had just come from the world will be overjoyed to see friends again and their friends overjoyed that they had arrived. When we enter the spiritual world, we have a body just as we have on this world. There seems to be no difference, since we don't see or feel any difference. This body is spiritual, however, since it has been purified from and separated from all earthly matter.

The body is the outer manifestation of our minds. The ancient Greek philosophers Plato and Augustine where dualist who believed the soul to be immortal. In fact, Socrates believed the soul is immortal and argued that death isn't the end of existence; it's merely separation of the soul from the body.

I remembered when my grandmother was on her death bed, all my relatives on my mother's side were there to support her transition. My mother asked her if she recognize everyone in the room. She looked up and said, "Yes, but who is that man over there in the corner of the room." As she looked, we also looked but saw no one. My grandmother said with a smile to the corner of the room where no one was standing, "I'm ready," and then she transitioned or passed away with a smile on her face. What a profound experience I witnessed. I learned from that experience that, although family was and can be around, you don't have to have family present, there will be spiritual beings assigned to support your transition, **NO ONE DIES ALONE!**

A veteran who was in hospice shared with me that when he had crossed over, he saw his pet dog who greeted him. He never thought that animals had souls. It took his religion to a whole new level. He stated that he was able to communicate with his pet through mental telepathy, that he was able to communicate to all life that way. In addition, there's no death there; nothing dies and there's no shadows because God's light is everywhere. Also, breathing isn't a requirement nor is eating. All living things are in heaven like on earth, plants and animals. Matthew 6:10 "As it is in heaven, so shall it be on earth."

One interesting thing a near-death experiencer shared with me about coming from source and being a part of the Creator is that we ask to come to this planet. In other words, we were beating the door down to come to this school of life to learn what joy is. Countless number of near-death experiencers shared the experience they had while in heaven, stating that we, as spirits, were aware of the obstacles and challenges, both mental and physical, that we were going to face before we came here, but we told our Creator to send us here anyway, knowing that we possessed the skills and power to overcome anything that comes our way. Many of us forgot that resolve once we're born because it's taught out of us by our parents and friends. So, earth becomes the school for us, and school is in session. Every time we fail a lesson, the Creator is there to help guide us through. He's the GPS system in our souls to redirect or recalculate us to fulfill our purpose while guiding us through the minefields of life.

In Plato's Republic, there's a story about a Greek warrior named Er who had a near-death experience. Er talked about seeing people in heaven lining up to come to this world. He saw all different patterns of lives people chose to go into such as criminals, doctors, holy persons, various forms of leadership, and so on. At the beginning of this line, were guides saying to each one as they passed by, "Whatever life you choose will not affect the quality of your soul." The guides said that life is a screenplay of illusions, that you play the part you took to be responsible for. Life and death are one, even as the river and sea are one.

Each event or tragedy we experience is a lesson to be learned. If we don't learn the lesson from the experience, our Creator loves us so much and doesn't want any of us to fail, so he gives us makeup quizzes. Often, we wonder why we see the same issue repeatedly. It's because God is trying to teach us that there's joy to be gain in every obstacle. We never appreciate success until we've failed. Success brings about joy. How good do we feel when we accomplish a goal or go through a challenge? And on the other side of that challenge, we feel the joy of a lesson learned. Trouble doesn't last long; it's a thing we pass through. If we can't pass the quizzes of life to get our joy, then we're unable to pass the test that's always coming. I hear my mother say, "This too shall pass." We're supposed to go through trouble, not establish residency in it. If we do, life then becomes a struggle of depression, addictions, physical challenges, marital problems, mental issues, relationship issues, you name it. The purpose of life is to learn how to love.

CHAPTER 3

I like to say that the real purpose of life is to enjoy life, just be happy. You want to get to a place where you aren't trying to get someplace else. Some people spend their entire lives, striving to be somewhere they're not. Then, even if they arrive, they don't know if that's where they're supposed to be. One of the ways to try to understand the purpose of your life is to return to nature, to find your own nature. All being originates in nonbeing. Jesus said it's the spirit that gives life, that you really don't come from your parents. All of us came from this place called spirit. That when you show up to this world from a tiny little drop of human protoplasm, a speck if you will, and everything in that little speck became you. I call it the future pill.

The avenue provided by the Creator to come to the planet is through the wombs of our mothers. While in our mother's womb as a small protoplasm of DNA, we had everything we needed. We never had to worry about anything: the color of our hair, the color of our skin, the shape of our bodies, the color of our eyes, even and most important mission, our purpose. All was taken care of because we were all perfect spiritual beings. The conflict comes at the time of our birth. I said it many times just as my parents said to God, "Lord, thank you for giving us this perfect child; you couldn't do any better. What a marvelous perfect gift you gave us. We'll take over from here." We're then taught by our parents how to live, what's right or wrong, whom we should love, what kind of job we should have, and what we need to do to be successful. So, then our purpose and who we are is being taught out of us. We knew why we came here, but now we're confused. So, immediately, ego becomes our friend and guide. We're told that we can't trust who we really are. We have to trust in something outside of ourselves, so we're on a journey for ambition. The ego, which is part of us, tells us that what we are isn't this perfect divine creation where we came from. No, the ego says that who we are is what we have. It begins with our toys, back accounts, and then our possessions. Before you know it, we began to identify ourselves with the amount of possessions we have. We spend the rest of our lives asking, Who am I? Why am I here? What am I supposed to be doing with my life? So, if you're a Christian, Jesus brings you back to your purpose; it's where the GPS begins after you experience a quantum moment. One of the gifts that our Creator gave us while in our mother's womb is a spiritual personality trait. This trait is designed to help direct us to our purpose or reason to be here on this planet. I call it a spiritual temperament trait.

There are four temperaments traits: (1) ruler, (2) designer, (3) promoter, and (4) server. These traits are seen in one's character and spiritually drives natural behaviors. It doesn't matter what your ethnic background is or what country you're from. It doesn't even matter what religion you follow; all humans have a spiritual trait that guides them to fulfill their purpose. A shift or quantum moment is important because it brings you back to purpose, back to your beginnings. These traits are distributed by God's design. Even though you may come from the same womb that your siblings came from, doesn't mean that you'll have the same spiritual trait. Disagreements are created simply because personality traits are clashing. These spiritual traits are given to us so that we can learn how to adjust, fit in, embrace, and love each over for growth. Let's examine these traits every human being has.

If you're born with a ruler spiritual trait, you like to be in charge and often take over leadership when things aren't going the way you think they should. Rulers are generally extroverted. As they speak, they're telling you what they think. There's no ambiguity or confusion in their explanations. They don't waste a lot of time being wordy. They get to the point quickly, and what they say seems to have little regard to the feelings of the listener. They are too busy making the point, and when that's established, they then become concerned about how you feel about it. They're task oriented. Rulers consistently make plans and complete projects through sheer determination. They are often oblivious to the cost to others, so they pursue their goals single-mindedly. They're practical and forceful, with strongly held opinions on the best way of doing things. Rulers can be prone to temper flare-ups when people don't meet their expectations. They may bitterly criticize others and then hold a grudge. However, despite this and because of their adeptness at martialing forces and their dogged perseverance, they can strongly motivate the workers in an organization. Eventually, however, unless they change their tactics, no one will be able to work with them. They make good "hired guns," but may be ineffective for long-term maintenance. Rulers get upset when talking with you and you start looking off as if you aren't interested or lose eye contact with them; they like to control your attention. On a bad day, they can be domineering, opinionated, impatient, and critical of those who have the gifts of mercy, teaching, and service. However, when a shift or a quantum moment happens in their lives, they are submitted to Christ and the brethren. They admit their imperfections. They're decisive, efficient, and enjoy challenges, refusing to quit. They're visionary and capable of inspiring others. When your speaking to them, you have to get to the point quickly because they have the tendency to cut you off from making your point because they believe that they know where you're going with your thought. The kinds of occupations these people look for and excel in are managers, lawyers, physicians, police officers, or firefighters. If they aren't doing any of these occupations, they are probably looking for another job.

If you're born with the designer spiritual temperament, you find it difficult to leave an incomplete project and would often lose sleep until it's done. You have a sensitivity to aesthetics; you create environments that are pleasing to the eye. You are known to be a jealous worker who is often a perfectionist and excel at analytical tasks. You often establish high standards for yourself and others. Your school grades often reflect high standards. You aren't easily swayed from your course of action but will persist even in the face of obstacles. I describe these people as the closest thing to a human computer. They often unconsciously close their eyes or rub their heads when speaking or making a point. They are always processing in their minds, trying to figure out how it makes sense. Just because you say a thing is right or wrong, doesn't mean that it is in their minds. These people are introverted, you never know what they're thinking unless they tell you.

Often, when you speak to them, they may be preoccupied by or thinking about a previous conversation or occurrence. They're task oriented; they have the tendency to be a perfectionist toward themselves and others. They're cautious when leading. They're pleased by attractive surroundings. If they're teachers, they possess the ability to stick with the listener until they completely understand. They can figure out that there's more than one way to feed a cat. At times, they're dominated with gifts of prophecy, teaching, and service. In the natural, they're perfectionistic and self-critical. They often beat themselves up with would have, could have, should have. The internal guilt bothers them for not being both thorough and quick, resulting in mood swings. They're judgmental, overly punitive, critical of those who demonstrate gifts of mercy, exhortation, and leadership. However, when a shift or quantum moment happens to them, they become aware that only the Creator is perfect, they become zealous, stable, artistic, and are respected for their self-sacrifice. The kinds of occupations these people look for and excel in are managers, accountants, engineers, architects, computer operators, scientists, mathematicians, lawyers, teachers, physicians, artists, writers, clerks, auto mechanics, and tradespeople. These people can adjust to any occupation to make it work. If they aren't careful, they can become workaholics.

If you're born with the spiritual temperament of a promoter, you already naturally have the ability to persuade. These people are known as "the life of the party" because of their genial wit, exuberance, and love for people. Their energy seems endless, and they inspire others to action, often optimistically predicting that everything will work out fine. These people are often highly compassionate toward others because they're affected by others needs and they share their feelings, often crying or laughing with them. As a child, their bedroom looked like the battle of Armageddon took place there. They have many imaginary friends and can play long periods of time alone. They are the jack of all trades and the master of none. This is because they have many incomplete projects due to their impulsiveness; they'll start another project without completing the one they are presently engaged with. They may have, at one point in their lives, been called the class clown. Promoters are very loyal in a relationship, even if it's bad or toxic. They find it difficult letting go for their sanity. People who are promoters are likely to encourage and edify others and less likely to put them down. They always see the glass half full and not half empty. As a child, children in the community are always hanging around their house waiting for them to come out and play. They love team sports and are uncomfortable having to work alone for long. Promotors often communicate by using their hands or body gestures to make a point. They often stretch the truth or lie to persuade you to their point of view. They make good salespeople or coaches. They have the tendency to recognize odd things, and, due to their impulsiveness, they say what they see out loud. For example, they may see a large lady and, without restraint, say out loud, "look at that fat lady over there!" They didn't have to say that, but because of their impulsiveness, they do. They're extroverted, people oriented, and are responsive to others' needs. Also, they are dominated by the spiritual gifts of mercy, exhortation, and leadership. In the natural, they tend to be egocentric, have wide mood swings, are disorganized, are prone to hasty decisions, and are critical of those who have the spiritual gifting of prophecy, teaching, and service. When a shift or quantum moment happens to them, they're submitted to the leadership of their Creator. They are attentive to others needs, disciplined, and dynamic in leadership. The kinds of occupations these people thrive in are managers, teachers, coaches, writers because of their imaginations, artist, entertainers, marketers, and salespeople.

If you're born with the spiritual temperament of a server, you appear to be calm and dependable and never seem to get excited about anything. You may appear cool and calm, but, inside, your spirit may be intense or anxious. As a child, it may have been difficult for you to ask a teacher for help while in a classroom setting. These people hate confrontations and try to avoid them at all cost. They're thinking *Why can't we all just get along?* These people cry at sad movies and are emotionally affected when they see tragedy. If they're in a group, they'd rather be a spectator than a participant. They love working behind the scenes and are uncomfortable with open recognition for their work. When these people tell you that they know how you feel, take it to the bank; they know exactly how you feel because they have the gift of empathy. They're extremely passionate toward others. Like a designer, these people keep thoughts to themselves and won't tell you what they really think. They believe doing this will save you any pain you might hear and avoid confrontations. They're introverted, people-oriented, and like to help out behind the scenes. They're dominated by the spiritual gifts of mercy, teaching, and service. In the natural, they're stressed by change of any kind. They find it difficult to look you in the eye when talking about a stressful situation. They're great procrastinators. They often are unable to rule their children because they want them to be happy, so they break their own rule of discipline. They are manipulated by loss of love. They can be critical of those who demonstrate gifts of prophecy, exhortation, and leadership. When a shift or quantum moment happens to them, they are very trusting in the Creator's faithfulness, they are diligently seeking the Creator's guidance, and they make excellent parents and love serving others. The kinds of occupations these people do well in are accountant, personnel officers, religious leaders, social workers, scientist, teachers, and health technicians.

In any given setting, we can operate on all the spiritual personality traits. But if you follow your gut instincts, the inner core that drives you, you'll make decisions that will bring satisfaction to your spiritual preference. For example, if you're working at a job that you get so much satisfaction and joy from that you feel you would do that job without pay, then that's your calling, and it's where God wants you to be. You're living out your spiritual personality trait gift. If you aren't happy at a job but only there because of the paycheck, then you're probably not where you need to be because it doesn't match your spiritual trait, resulting in you looking for another job. You want to always be looking for your preferred setting for satisfaction.

As a chaplain working at the Veteran Affairs hospital, I was able to witness the operation of the various spiritual personalities play itself out with family members of a dying veteran. The veteran patient who was dying was on a respirator, and it was only a matter of time before he passed. I was called in to minister to the family and help them process their grief. This veteran had six children and they were in the waiting lounge arguing about when they should pull the plug on Daddy. One of his children seemed to have a ruler spiritual personality. He immediately said, "I think we should pull the plug." He wanted to end the misery and move on. He saw no reason to have his father hang around until the inevitable. The patients second oldest seemed to have a designer spiritual personality trait. She chimed in, stating that she couldn't see medically that there was any hope of bringing Daddy back, so she agreed with the older brother. The third and fourth child appeared to have a promoter spiritual personality. They responded by saying, "Just because it's the right thing to do doesn't mean that we ought to do it now. Let's see if Daddy improves. Let's not put him in the grave yet." These kids were hanging onto hope. The last two children were sobbing and didn't engage in the conversation. They wanted their father to stay on the respirator because they couldn't emotionally embrace the reality that their father wasn't coming back. So, this decision process went on for three days. The ruler and designer children were angry because the other four siblings didn't agree with them, so they couldn't decide. Eventually, their father died when the respirator flatlined. It appeared that Daddy made the decision for them.

While a chaplain, one of my responsibilities was to facilitate spirituality groups among patients, and I saw firsthand how the various spiritual personality traits operated in a group setting. I gave the group a task to come up with a plan on how to use the pay phone in the hallway. The first persons to speak were my ruler patients. They talked about what had to be done. My designer patients explained how it was to be done in detail. The problem came with my promoter patients. Their position was just because there was a solution doesn't mean that everybody is comfortable with it, so they wanted to talk about it more. When it wasn't about the solution, it was about the fellowship. They loved to engage in discussions and, most likely, to hear themselves talk. My rulers quickly recognized the filibustering and responded by saying we had already resolved the problem, there's nothing else to talk about, so let's move on. My designer patients were thinking, *Maybe we haven't looked at all the possibility; we must have missed something.* My server patients didn't say anything because they don't like confrontations anyway; they prefer being in a spectator's role rather than a participant. They prefer to be like a fly on the wall observing the chaos. They'll usually respond by saying, "When you guys make a decision, let me know," and they leave the room because the environment is too intense for them to be present.

Personally, I witness some of the spiritual personality traits operate in my own household with my family. My former wife's spiritual personality trait is a designer. She was always good with handling the finances and general operations of the household. Any plans for the family had to make sense for her to process what needed to be done to bring about the family activity. Being a promoter myself, I was too impulsive in the decision-making process. I made a decision based upon the way it made everybody feel. My ex-wife would always say that I was inefficient in running the household. So, I let her plan the outing, and after she brought the results to me, then I would decide from her recommendations. My oldest Corbi and my youngest Aaron both have promoter spiritual personality traits. Both have many friends, some imaginary and some not; they can play for a long time alone and their bedrooms look like the battle of Armageddon took place there. I witness children in the neighborhood hanging around our house, waiting for Aaron to come out to play as though they couldn't play without him. Corbi lived in two households, mine and her mother's, so she had the best of both worlds and was enjoying that status because she could make friends anywhere. Now, my daughter Mikaela has a ruler spiritual personality trait. She likes to be in charge and would take the leadership role immediately through forced persuasion. I witness her with her friends who started out playing the game they wanted to play but quickly wound up playing the games Mikaela wanted to play. That happed often. The Bible says train a child up the way they should go and they will no depart from it. Well, knowing my children's personality traits, I was able to put them in sports that matched their traits.

Aaron and Corbi played team sports. They excelled because they loved the team concept. It didn't matter for them if they won or lost; it was about the competition and fellowship. Mikaela was different, she didn't like team sports because she wasn't in control over her teammates; she played with an angry spirit. But when she was put in the sport of tennis, she excelled. It was a sport where she was in control and didn't have to depend on anyone but herself. She once told me that if I got too old to handle or be on my own, she would put me in a nursing home and pay for around-the-clock care for me because she had no patience to take care of me. Of course, her siblings who have promoter traits would love for me to live with them until my last days. Academically, my son Aaron and my daughter Corbi did will in English and history because they had story lines, but continue to struggle in analytical task, but Mikaela did well in technical subjects like math and science. So, I expected to see high grades in math and science. Aaron and Corbi I expected to see high grades in English and history. If any of my promoter children brought in a C for math and science, it was looked upon as an A. For Mikaela, although history and English were challenging, she strove for excellence getting all A's. She was even challenging the teacher's syllabus while in college, saying their teaching methods were unsatisfactory.

It was also interesting at the dinner table. I watched my ex-wife, who loves order, try to organize the conversation at the dinner table between the children. My two promoter children would start talking about any subject trying to see who could outtalk or share who had the better story while my ruler child, who likes to get to the point and not waste time by being wordy, said what she wanted to say early on, got up from the table, and was gone. She didn't want to engage in a conversation of nonsense as she saw it.

CHAPTER 4

A clear shift in thinking is seen in near-death experiencers who add new meaning to life. The more people who experience NDEs, the more transformative this world becomes. This experience is designed to create heaven here on earth. This is one way God is transforming mankind. What slows the process is man's ability to choose. God doesn't bind a man's will. He created man with the ability to choose. The only thing that separates us from the angels is the ability to choose. Man chooses and has to face the consequences of his choice. Ego drives selfish decisions, which, in turn, harms others. You would be surprised at how many people you effect on the other side of the world by the decisions you make here and vice versa. It's like dropping a rock in the lake an seeing the ripple effects from that rock. Whatever you throw out in the heavens comes back to you. Some say it karma or what goes around comes around. You reap what you sow. This is a universal truth on how the spiritual world we live in works.

One of the most polarizing ideologies of mankind is the belief in a religion. Wars have started based on religion. Man is willing to scorch the earth in the name of the god of their faith. I find that the most segregated time in our country is on Sunday morning. We have allowed religion to separate and divide us as a human race with the false idea that one's religion is the right way and everyone else is wrong. Religion can be rigid in its beliefs, making it difficult to be open to possibilities of acceptance. I was watching a movie, *The Book of Eli,* which showed a world that had been devastated by war over the Bible and religion. So they found all religious books, including the Bible and had them destroyed so there would be no more wars. Although that movie was fiction, we are living in a world where

1at could be a possibility. This world is made up of many different religions 1d all have their place and serve a purpose for mankind. Religion brings us ope and encouragement. The problem comes when we get caught up with 1e misinterpretation of a holy book's content. I hear very often that the ible or other holy book has flaws, and that's why people don't read or elieve in a holy book. But all holy books are spiritually inspired by the riter through the influence of the Creator, resulting in its perfection and awlessness. The imperfection is from the interpretation of the reader, not 1e book. Religion gives you a moral foundation and keeps you centered 1d focused with the goal of maximizing your potential. Religion is man's earch for God or a higher power. It's a constant quest to find and connect rith your Creator. However, spirituality is the sensitivity or attachment to eligious values. Spirituality brings life to religion. It takes religion to the ext level of your relationship with God. Every human being is a spiritual eing. Our souls are spiritual. The essence of unlimited power is given to very human being by the Creator. It has no barrier to race, social status, thnic origin, it has no culture monopoly, and it's colorless; spirituality mbraces all. God is a spirit and he created humans out of himself from rhich we as the human race came. Without the spirit of our Creator, we on't exist. Because we're spiritual beings and God is a spiritual entity, we're 1e big family. So, God, whom I call the Creator, is in everything and is verywhere. There's no place or time where he is not. He's in the very air we reathe. So, this spirit, this power, this energy goes from everlasting to verlasting. It has no beginning and it has no end. It's eternal and because 's eternal, we are eternal.

One veteran shared with me his near-death experience he had as a pilot. Ie said that he was about to land a plane and upon his approach to the nding something had gone wrong and the wings on the plane hit the mway and he began to slide out of control. He said the moment when that

appened, he left his body and saw himself on the outside of the plane atching the drama of the crash. He said the oddest thing about watching 1e crash was he found himself looking from the standpoint of every piece

of gravel that was being kicked up by the plane, and this seemed spirituall
natural for him at that time. He was able to experience the crash, watch th
crash from different perspectives at the same time, and feel in harmony witl
it. This spiritual experience he called being omnipresent everywhere at th
same time. He stated that it was the weirdest experience he had ever had.

When we cross over, our senses will be heighten one hundred times
Feelings of guilt or shame and even mental or physical ailments disappeas
Many near-death experiencers stated that they saw a panoramic view of thei
life but only events that demonstrated caring for others and where the
could have done better with the opportunity to help someone's life to be
little better. It seems that God wipes away all negative events and put then
in the sea of forgetfulness. They also shared that for all the people they hur
in their lives, they felt the pain they caused magnified one hundred times. I
felt to them that they were in judgment. Nearly all near-death experiencer
stated that they didn't see God physically but felt and saw his present in th
light and in everything that surrounded them. This light and source o
energy was full of love and forgiveness. Some had shared that when you ar
where God is, there are no shadows because of the light emanating from hi
power. Nothing dies there, so no death is there but only life in its fullness
Those who treat others badly have already made their choice to separat
themselves from this life, resulting in a hell experience or destiny. One clien
of mine shared his hell experience and was glad that he was resuscitated b
his doctors after he had flatlined on the operating table during heart surgery
He stated that his experience was so intense and frightening that it took hin
a whole year to calm down to be able to talk about it. He shared hov
demons pulled his arm off and started beating him with it and he felt all th
pain. They ripped open his skin and poured fecal matter in him; that pain h
couldn't escape. His spiritual body would grow back, and they would do i
again and again, getting great joy, seeing him scream and suffer. He wishe
he could die but being in a spiritual state, he couldn't. It's understood is
religious circles that people who are in pain and decide to commit suicide t
escape the pain go to hell where they cannot escape pain, and there, the pais
is magnified for all eternity. He stated that he learned while you're in you

spiritual body, there are no pain receptors. For example, if you hurt your finger in your physical body only your finger hurts. But when you're in your spiritual body, everything hurts; you feel it everywhere with the same intensity. He said following that experience, he'll never say to anyone "Go to hell." Hell wasn't made for humans, but many of us choose to go there for the belief that the Creator doesn't exist. Ego says we don't need God the Creator. All we need is ourselves and our lucky breaks. It would be a shame living our whole lives and, at the end of life on your death bed, asked the question it you had lived right or if God exists at all. Believe it or not, you're going to find out; it's best to be safe and lose nothing than to gamble and lose everything.

CHAPTER 5

An unseen spiritual power is all around us to assist in fulfilling our purpose. I'm a *Star Wars* fan, and the main character in *Star Wars* is Luke Skywalker. His mentor Obi Wan Kenobi told him to use the force, that all-powerful spirit or energy that flows all around and binds us together. This power isn't transcendent or seen as the man upstairs. This divine love of energetic consciousness is everywhere. Our human DNA is made of this energetic consciousness and can feel this power during times of meditation and prayer. We came from it and are created by it. Like the air we breathe, we can't see it, but we can feel it because it's a part of us. The story was told about a little boy flying a kite with a long string on it. It flew so high in the sky the clouds covered it. A man came by and asked the little boy what he was doing. The boy answered, "I'm flying a kite." The man said to the little boy, "I don't see a kite and how do you know it's there?" The little boy said, "Every now and then, I feel a tug on the string that lets me know it's still there." That's what our Creator does for us. When we think he isn't there or not concern about us, he pulls on the string of our heart, feelings and experiences, to let us know he's there.

I'm also a *Star Trek* fan and had an interesting observation about that show: the starships have no chaplains. It seems that chaplains or pastors are written out of movie scripts of the future. They don't seem to be important or have any value anymore. About 95% of humans on this planet believe in a higher power of some sort. Religion today has become a threat to the nonbelievers of our communities. However, spirituality is acceptable and seems to be nonthreatening because it doesn't focus on any particular religion or faith group. I remember as a child asking my father what was the right religion to choose. He told me a story about five blind men who were each asked to touch an elephant and describe what he felt. One blind man described the trunk, another blind man described the tail, another described a leg, yet another described the side, and the last described the elephant's ear. So, my father began to explain that all the blind men had a piece of the elephant but no one had the whole thing. So, whatever religion you choose is the right one for you. It's the inner pulling of our Creator, which draws you to your preferred faith path to connect with him. So, religion becomes man's search for the Creator. Spirituality is the connection to the Creator or sensitivity to his inner promptings.

In the spiritual world, things work exactly opposite to the natural world. For example, if you want to receive you have to give. If you want to have friends you have to show yourself friendly. If you want to be served, you must serve others first. It's important to understand that it's not how much you love but how much you are loved by others.

One of the ways to be loved by others is to live a lifestyle of forgiveness. Many people of faith aren't clear on how this forgiveness process works. Some believe time heals all wounds, yet they think avoiding the person or issue helps. The problem with addressing forgiveness that way is that it doesn't give account to the feelings that are connected with the situation. You may say you forgive but you'll never forget; this is because feelings are involved, and trust has been destroyed. When we ask God to forgive us, we believe he puts the issue in the sea of forgetfulness. We, as spiritual beings, possess the same ability to do just that. We have the power to overcome any past hurts that prevent us from going forward with our lives. So, then the question is, "How do we forgive?" the act of forgiveness is a spiritual act of the will. You have to decide to forgive; you cannot just feel the need to forgive. If that were the case, you'll never feel the need because you want that person to pay or suffer like you did. Feelings get in the way of the process of addressing the issue. When someone ask you to forgive them, it's because some trust has been destroyed and needs to be rebuilt or restored. So, what we're looking for is something to hold that person accountable, a way to rebuild trust. However, if that person comes to you and says, "Forgive me, and this is what I'm going to do to change my behavior," and they begin to give you an honest list, that will get your attention immediately because they gave you something to work with that will hold them accountable. This process will restore trust over a short time. Likewise, give that person something to hold you accountable to as well. Now you're working the forgiveness process. An important note about this process is that you do it without looking for anything in return. Some people won't release you because they're hurting, but you do the process because God is pleased with your spiritual growth and it's the right thing to do. Don't let your ego lock you in a box of pride and selfishness.

The other difficulty we have and struggle with is forgiving ourselves for past negative behaviors. This process works in three phases. In the first phase, you should write a letter about an issue you struggle with. Once you write it, read it; you'll be amazed by how much effect it has on your feelings when you see it in print. Then throw the letter away. That's the physical way of throwing it into the sea of forgetfulness. Write another letter and throw it away; keep doing that until you get the results you want. Talking about it and not seeing it written won't have an effect on you by itself. Secondly, pray to God about it; he can handle your mess even if you don't package it right. He understands, so pray constantly and get it out of you. When you keep your guilt and shame inside, they'll take you through depression, anxiety, and fear, not where you want to go. Thirdly, talk to someone about the issue. You aren't looking for a response necessarily; you're just trying to get it out of you. Be careful with whom you share it with because trust is very important here. Usually, these persons are your best friends or your counselor, just someone who will listen with no feedback or judgments. When you do those three things, what you'll discover is that you'll no longer feel bad about the issue. It will no longer hook you with guilt or shame about would have, should have, could have. You test the comfortability about it when someone brings it up. If it no longer upsets you, that will be your sign that you've finally forgiven yourself. That's a piritual exercise that brings about deliverance. No medications, legal or onlegal, can remove your guilt. It's the only process that works with the ower we already have through our Creator.

The closer we get to our Creator, the more we lose our ego. It's the law of hysics that only one thing can occupy one space at a time. It would be either our ego or your relationship with the Creator. This decision is easily made ter a quantum moment experience. When ego is no longer the driving force your life, only then can you realize that there's a powerful organized force at's in all things designed to work for you, almost as if you were making it appen just by being connected to the Creator. So, then, the destiny outside f yourself is no longer important or the relative driving force in your life. ou're connected to the Source, the Creator. It's almost like this divine telligence seems to be saying, "You play your music, and I'll help you deal ith any obstacle that comes your way." It's not going to be any trouble for ou because the Creator is supporting you. All of us come here to play this usic or fulfill purpose. We don't have to live up to someone else's xpectation, but we must live out what we came here to do.

A shift or quantum moment can happen in many ways. It could be a omment, an event, an experience when you shift from ego, when you allow ourself to live from a divine source of peace called spirit. We begin living om what I call the virtues of life. There are four of them: (1) reverence for l life, respect all things; (2) sensitivity, a sense of honesty; (3) gentleness, racticing kindness to others; and lastly, (4) supportiveness, servicing others. ou can ask, "What's my purpose?" You'll always find it in serving others.

When a shift happens, in that moment, your values are turned upside own. Men and women experience the shift differently. Before the shift or uantum moment, men valued:

1. wealth - making as much money as they can
2. a sense of adventure - seeing the world, exploring
3. achievement - accomplishing something, you are what you do attitude
4. seeking pleasure - doing what feels good
5. respect - wanting to be respected, fighting

Look what happens after the shift or quantum moment:
1.   spirituality is very important - getting closer to the Creator
2.   personal peace - happy with self, contentment
3.   family – protection, keeper of the gate, covering over 4. wanting to d¢
Gods will - fulfilling purpose 5. honesty - being open with feelings.

Before the shift or quantum moment women valued:
1. family - taking care of the family, being a good mother
2. having a sense of independence - don't need anyone, self-reliance
3. career - job security
4. fitting in - needing to be liked, being like everyone else.
5. attractiveness - how do I look, appearance

After the shift or quantum moment:
1. concern about own personal growth
2. a sense of self-esteem - self worth
3. spirituality - connection to the Creator or source
4. happiness - comfortable with self, satisfied with self
5. forgiveness - releasing pass hurts

CHAPTER 6

In this section, I want to talk about the reception of thought. In Matthew 16:15, Jesus asked the disciples "Whom do men say that I am?" and Peter responded by saying, "Thou are the Christ, Son of the living God." Jesus said then to Peter, "Flesh and blood did not reveal this to you but my father in heaven." In other words, that thought didn't originate from you, nor was it created by your brain. That thought was downloaded to Peter from the Creator himself, God. Our brains are receptors of thought and information. They don't create thought but receive thought. The brain is like a radio receiver. Whatever thought is circling around in the vortex of your mind, you focus on it and bring that thought into reality. Just as with TV, the only time it works is when it's turned on. When you do that, it receives the wave links in the air, and you see a picture. When you focus on godly thoughts, you're driven to do godly things; as a man thinketh, so is he. Your thoughts are spiritual communications and memories floating around in the vortex of your mind. Once you focus on a thought, you immediately choose how you'll feel about that thought. At that point, you began to bring that thought to reality. It's very important to understand that in the vortex of your thoughts, if you focus on the negative events that happen to you in the past, that's where you'll live. The apostle Paul said in Philippians 3:1314, "Brethren, I count not myself to have arrived, but this one thing that I am able to do, forget the things that are in my past and I look forward towards what is ahead. I press towards the goal to win the prize for which God has called me." In other words, those who put their hand to the plow and look back aren't fit for the kingdom of heaven. When you look back at your past negative experiences, you'll begin to live there. So, the things you should go through in a day may take you several months. Do not establish residency in your past. It's not bad to visit your past as a motivator or inspiration for the future, but don't live there. Learning how to meditate regularly helps you to shut out negative thoughts and clears your mind. How often have you found it difficult to fall asleep when you're thinking about pass experiences or events? A lifestyle of meditation will address that issue. Dr. Eben Alexander has created a tool called sacred acoustics, which helps to turn off the outside world and clear your mind.

Do some aspects of our personality survive bodily death? This question became the subject of scientific research by Dr. Bruce Greyson MD from the university of Virginia. He had followed up on a 50-year research study in the division of perceptional studies. During his research, he found that the brain is separate from the mind and that a transition happens when one dies; it separates. The brain is physical whereas the mind or consciousness is spiritual. In other words, the brain and consciousness aren't the same. You're part of and connected to the body, but your mind/consciousness and soul goes back to the Creator. Dr. Greyson shared one of his interesting studies about a woman who had a doctorate in mathematics and was teaching at a local collage. One day, while on her way to work, she was in a car accident. She suffered some head trauma. When they X-rayed her head, they discovered that she had no brain on the c-scan. When they opened her head, all they found was a brain stem used for body functioning but not thought. How could she function without a brain? Other studies with the same results happen to children who had high IQs with a severe case of hydrocephalies or water-filled brain cavity. Since they shouldn't be functioning at that high level of IQ, his conclusion was that the brain doesn't create thought but is a receptor of thought from a nonphysical realm.

When I was in grade school, my friends and I would play games while competing against each other. When one of us lost the game, we would always say, "Do over." That would give us another opportunity to change the outcome in our favor. You can imagine that these games would go on until our mothers called us in for dinner. When I look at people who had neardeath experiences or an out-of-body experience and were able to come back and talk about the lessons they learn from the experience, what I assume is that it's a "do-over." This spiritual journey that I've been on has taken me to a whole new level of clinical clarity and understanding.

One curious study that Dr. Greyson explored was provoked by a common understanding of some cultures where rebirth or reincarnation happens from time to time. However, there's no biblical basis for this understanding. So, Dr. Greyson started his research to address this phenomenon by doing a study on children who remember past lives. The hypothesis was that if consciousness is produced by the brain, then when the brain dies, consciousness ends; it cannot continue in another incarnation. So, if some of us do remember our past lives, thoughts and memory cannot reside solely in the brain. Dr. Ian Stevenson, Dr. Greyson mentor, did a 50-year study on very young children who claim to have memories of their past lives. Most of These children live in societies that have cultural beliefs in rebirth or re-incarnation. A great many of those children Dr Stevenson studied lived in India. To study these children Dr. Stevenson traveled many times to remote villages throughout India to interview these children and their families. However, Dr. Greyson and his team studied over 2,416 cases in Asia with children between the ages of 2-5 years old who spontaneously started talking about events of their past lives. In 60% of these cases, They gave enough detail so that their previous embodiment could be identified. the average age of death in the past life was around 33, but that varied from country to country. In places like the United States and Europe, where there's less violence and health care is more available, the age tended to be older. In 60% of the cases, the past life remembered ended violently, either in a tragic accident or by intentional wounding. The average time that passed between the death and the birth in the present life is 12 years, but that varies in keeping with cultural beliefs. For example, among the Jews in Lebanon, the children tended to be born immediately upon their death in a past life, which is in keeping with their cultural beliefs. As you might expect, these cases aren't easy to investigated. These children investigated had memories of distant places about people they had never met and had no knowledge of their existence. They mentioned names and occupations of relatives and friends in their past life and offered specific details of how that past life ended. In many cases, Dr. Greyson could take that child to a village they had never seen or visited but they could tell him all about places and landmarks they remembered from their past life. These children exhibited some unusual personality traits, likes, and dislikes that were incompatible with their present life. For example; some of these children had a past life of the opposite gender and wanted to dress and play like the opposite gender. A child born to a Hindu family recalled a past life as a Muslim and rejected the food his mother cooked because it wasn't prepared in the Muslim manner. Several Burmese children clamed to remember lives as Japanese who were shot down over Burma in WWII. They rejected the spicy Burmese foods and requested Japanese foods of raw fish. They also rejected the traditional Burmese clothes and wanted pants like the Japanese wore. Many children who recalled past lives had fears related to their past lives. For example, a child recalled being drowned in a well and had an unusual fear of being around water. Finally, these children were observed to have unusual skills that they hadn't been taught. For example, a child had the ability to play a musical instrument without being taught or had skills related to their occupation in their past life. In many cases, some of these children had birth defects attributed to their past lives. These birthmarks or birth defects matched death wounds of past lives. That occurred in about one third of the children investigated. Sometimes, the birthmarks faded as the children grew-up, but in other cases, they didn't. And, of course, birth defects persisted throughout the child's life. In 18% of these cases, they were able to confirm through medical records and autopsy reports that the death wounds from the past life did indeed correspond to the birthmarks or birth defects in the child's life. For example, the hands of a Burmese child were underdeveloped. She had no fingers. She remembers a life as a man, riding a bicycle on his way home when he was stopped by a gang who had been hired to kill him. They made him get down on his knees and prepared to cut off his head with the sword, but at the last moment, he suddenly raised his hands to plea for mercy or maybe to protect his face from the sword and the fingertips of his hands were cut off by the sword. As a child, this girl insisted on wearing boy clothes and referring to her actions in masculine verbal forms.

Dr. Greyson had an impressive case from a Christian family in the United States who had no prior knowledge of rebirth or reincarnation. Certainly, they had no interest or belief in this sort of thing. For Christians, there's no biblical basis to support a rebirth. A two-year-old boy by the name of James Lysander who was born in Louisiana seem to remember being shot down in the South Pacific Ocean in WWII nearly 60 years earlier. The boy would often play with airplanes and wake up screaming from a nightmare about being trapped in an airplane that was on fire. When he was three years old, his mother bought him a toy plane and pointed out what she thought were bombs on the airplane wings. But little James corrected her by saying, "Those aren't bombs; they're drop tanks," something she hadn't heard of. He eventually gave more details of his past life, saying he flew an airplane called a Corsair that used to get flat tires frequently, something that a military historian confirms would often happen. He also reported that the aircraft carrier he flew from was the USS Potomac, that he was killed flying over Iwo Jima, and that his best friend was another pilot named Jack Larson. Now, little James's father was a policeman and devout Baptist and was quite opposed to the possibility of reincarnation or rebirth. He researched the story in an attempt to discredit it. Instead, he found out that there was an aircraft carrier named the USS Potomac Bay at the battle of Iwo Jima in 1945 and that only one aircraft pilot was shot down in that battle. The pilot's name was James Huston. When his plane was shot down, it caught on fire. The little boy's parents tried to find the pilot's family. They eventually found the pilot's sister who lived in California about 3,000 miles away. She confirmed that her dead brother, James Huston, did have a friend named Jack Larson. And the little boy began to recognize several objects in the home that belonged to her dead brother. She was convinced that this little boy was the reincarnation of her dead brother.

So, in summary, there's abundant evidence of life and scientific research that the brain under extraordinary circumstances seems to come unlinked from consciousness, that consciousness functions better without the mediation of a functional brain. This evidence isn't accepted by most medical or scientific authorities. In fact, it's not known to most scientist. Nevertheless, it's there; it's reliable evidence.

One of the problems medicine/science has with spirituality is that it cannot be explained medically. To the world of science, spirituality is witchcraft or hocus pocus fantasy. Many physicians get angry when their patients share with them a near-death experience. To the patient, it's a very profound experience that changes their life dramatically and, on many occasions, heals them. When this happens, the medical community calls it spontaneous regeneration. The NDE doesn't fit the scientific model. To them it's just the results of a brain losing oxygen, causing hallucinations. So, the patient shuts up and doesn't tell anybody what they experienced. Even sharing their experience with religious folks can be a challenge. Religious folks believe in heaven and hell but don't believe it's possible to go there and come back to talk about it. There's no written record of Lazarus who died and was resurrected by Jesus sharing where he went before his resurrection. It would be nice to talk with him about his near-death experience. John on the island of Patmos stated that he was caught up into the third heaven and saw unspeakable things. The experience for him was very much like other near-death experiences. It was hard to put into words what he saw. You cannot put into words things you've never seen before by using worldly words.

Spirituality is beyond the reach of medicine or science. I haven't been able to find one scientist or doctor who can start the first sentence of how to create a cell or manufacture a thought. Some things are beyond medicine or scientific knowledge.

There's a difference between a near-death experience and an out-of-body experience. Near-death experience is triggered by trauma or fatal condition when the body is being shocked or compromised by an event. To have an out-of-body experience, you don't have to die or experience any traumatic experience. People who've had OBEs may be meditating, praying, or doing a simple task when they're taken out of their bodies to a different dimension or different realm. John the disciple of Jesus was taken up to the third heaven. A study of this shows that there are three levels of the heaven John was talking about. The first level, we call the troposphere (the sky/clouds). The second heaven is the stratosphere (the layer of the Earth's atmosphere above the troposphere, extending about 32 mile above the Earth's surface). The mesosphere is space.

Frank Wiess had experienced an out-of-body experience while standing in his kitchen at about 3am, getting a glass of water when he was taken out of his body and found himself in a hell dimension. He stated that while there, all memory of him being a Christian was taken from him as he sat in a cell with two demons who hated his existence. He said that these demons were fourteen feet high. He was asked how he knew they were that tall. He said that all communications were done through mental telepathy. You merely have to think a question and the answer would come back to you as though you spoke it out loud. All communications are done through telepathy in the spiritual world. The demons in the cell with him began to beat on him with great satisfaction, saying over and over to him, "We got you; we got you." What a horrifying experience; he had no power or strength to stop them. When he was able to return to his body, his memory of being a Christian was given back to him, and he asked God why he sent him there. He stated that God told him that a lot of people don't believe in hell so his mission now was to tell and teach people that hell is for real and that they don't want to go there. Hell is only designed for people who want to go there as a result of the decisions they make. Predestination is determined by the decisions we make. No one consciously makes decisions to go to hell, but the ego helps move the process along.

One of the struggles as spirits in a body is anger. The Bible says, "Be angry but sin not. Let not the sun go down without addressing your anger." It's very important to address anger because it can take you out of character. When you're angry, you're out of control. Very often, people ask me what am I to do with this spirit called anger? Anger is a gift from God. Anytime you don't understand the purpose of a thing, you'll abuse and misuse it. The proper use of this gift is to help you to recognize what has been an idol/god in your life. There are three areas that the ego creates as a god: relationships, property, and ideas (the way we think). When we get angry, it falls in one of these categories. Let's take relationships for example: How often are we angry with family members or associates because they did us wrong. Or perhaps a close family member dies, and we become angry because that relationship has been devalued. Any time your god (relationship) has been devalued, you aren't a happy camper about it. God the Creator is greater than your relationships. Your anger now isn't being used properly as a gift to determine what has been a god in your life, but is being used to separate you from a relationship with God. This is an indictment upon the lack of relation you have with your Creator. Anger is your idol detector to let you know that your relationships have been more important and have replaced God.

Let's look at property; how many people were committing suicide when the stock market fell? Or they became angry when their possessions were lost. They became insecure and depressed. What does God do for us? He provides a sense of security and comfort. When that's gone, people lose their purpose for living and forget that God our Creator provides our means for living. God says, "I'll provide all of your needs." When you lose your money, you lose yourself.

Finally, our ideas and the way we think. Sometime, we think that we're God. Anytime someone challenges the way we think, we become angry. God the Creator says that he's greater than you because he created you. Don't be so depressed when someone defiles you or defames you. Jesus said they will hate you because of him. So, anger is your idol detector to be used as a gift from the Creator. It's okay to be angry, but don't allow anger to feed into your ego because it will take you out of character and you'll be unable to fulfill your purpose. Don't let your anger become an indictment upon your personal relationship or lack of relationship with your Creator.

Because we are spiritual being, all emotions are driven by the spiritual world. We're in control on how we respond to external stimuli. All feelings we experience are controlled by choice. If you're angry or depressed, it's because you chose to be. Who told you that you had to feel that way? A lot of external stimuli are designed for you to make an emotional decision. Just as it is when we feel happy or joyful, we chose to feel that way. Choices always have consequences. Many people chose to be happy in the midst of adversity. Life's school is in session and there are daily quizzes to pass.

CHAPTER 7

Genesis 2:7 KIV: "And the Lord God formed man out of the dust of the ground and breathed into his nostrils life and man became a living soul." The Creator breathed himself into us to exist. This means that we don't exist without God's spirit in us. I often use an example of a glove. If a glove is on a table, it doesn't move on its own. Why because it has no power of life to function. It's just a glove, an inanimate object. But if I put my hand in that glove, it becomes full of life and is dictated by my will to move it. My hand represents the spirit of the Creator. It brings power and energy to move and function. Once my hand is out of the glove, it ceases to function or move. it has no desire or power to move on its own. So, when our spirit leaves our body, our body ceases to function and our spirit/soul goes back to the Creator who gave it life. Our soul/consciousness is housed in our spirit or energy. We are represented by God who has a higher intelligence with immense, unlimited power. That DNA is in all of us who were born to this world. To make this clear, let me use this following example: If a pie were on the table and I cut a slice out of the pie, that slice doesn't cease being a pie; it's a piece of the pie. That piece has all the ingredients that are in the whole pie. So, we're a part of the whole, which is God himself. We possess the same abilities that the Creator has because we're a part of him. We are of the Creator, so the Creator exists. To say he doesn't exist is to say we don't exist. Because the Creator is spirit, we are spirit hands housed in these gloves called bodies. Like the natural leather or cloth of a glove, a body wears out over time. We are here in this life for a short time to fulfill our purpose, then we return to God our Creator. Yes, our bodies wear down; aches and pains are signs that all good things must come to an end. We aren't here forever. The only thing that

ves forever is our spirit, our consciousness, our sense of awareness. That's
ecause the Creator lives forever. He has no beginning and no end. He
xists forever, so we exist forever. We cannot die spiritually; only our body
ies. It ceases to function or exist, but our souls, our spirits, our
onsciousness lives forever. Physical death is only our transition to the life
ternal. Your body dies after your spirit leaves and not before. That's when
ie transition takes place; we leave this physical state and transition to a
piritual state in which we're free from the limitations of the body. We leave
three-dimensional world and transition to a fifth-dimensional world of the
pirit. Jesus called this world paradise. In the Gospel of Luke 23:43, he told
ne of the malefactors on the cross, "This day, you will be with me in
aradise." Death isn't the end of life but the beginning. So, until then, the
uestion becomes: What have you done while here on this planet to fulfill
our mission before you go home to the Creator?

We are spiritual beings having human experiences. Because we are
piritual beings, it's very difficult but not impossible to do heavenly acts of
ealing, loving, showing compassion for others, and practicing random acks
f kindness. These acts we are truly capable of doing. It's in the Creator's
)NA, so it's in our DNA. But many of us choose not to because we live in
ι ego-driven world.

When you're able to overcome your ego, the spirit motivates you
aturally to demonstrate its attributes. These spiritual attributes are
ianifested by acts of love, joy, peace, patience, kindness, goodness,
iithfulness, gentleness, and self-control. By embracing the ability to look
iward for guidance, God will show himself strong. Making decisions based
pon the way we think will always lead to our downfall. Proverbs chapter
3:7 reads, "As a man thinketh in his heart so is he." Whatever you focus on
ι the vortex of your thoughts happens. Because the Creator can create, so
an we. When you focus on a negative thought, you began to create the
tmosphere for that thought to become a reality. All thoughts are spiritual in
ieir origin. You can't see a thought. It isn't made of matter; it isn't physical
r something you can reach out and touch. It has no form or texture; it's a
)irit. All things that you see in the physical come from and are created by

the spiritual. You think about it and then you figure out how to bring tha thought into reality. You think, you say, and then you do. The written wore gives us an example. In the first 22 chapters of Genesis, God said, and afte his statement, something happened. He said a word, which is spiritual, ane creation came to pass. When we speak, we bring about our reality? I ofte tell people who are in addictions that if you stand up at an AA/NA meetin and say, "I am an addict," they will have sealed their fate because in the spiritual world of words, they create all the reasons they need to be in thei addiction. But if they stand up in that same meeting and say, "I am recovering addict," they'll always be sober because recovery is sobriety Anything you voice becomes that reality. Proverbs 18:21 reads, "Death ane life are in the power of the thought." What we've said in the past as a peopl has resulted in our social immorality and chaos. Those who use profanit create an environment that's profane.

In every human being, there's an inner core, the true self, which consistently pulls us through life and its experiences. It's our guide tha helps us fulfill our purpose. This inner core is our gut instincts, ou intuition, the still small voice of our God. It knows what you need and hov to get it. What you need is out there in the spiritual world trying to find yor so that you and your core can meet up and have mutual benefit from the union. Humility is possessing the ability to put the way you think and fee aside, open yourself up to direction, and following that direction with trus that you'll get your desired results. If you can do that, you'll always be at the right place at the right time. After asking for guidance and using my faith a the runway of my decision-making prosses, I followed my gut feelings ane began making decisions of core satisfaction.

One night, I went to a restaurant called "Catfish Dewy." I often gr there to eat crawfish. This particular night, it had all you can eat crawfish or the menu. I felt the strong need to sit at the bar, since I didn't have to wai long if I sat there. So, I made the gut decision, with satisfaction I might add to sit there. As I was sitting there, a man who was clearly inebriated startee arguing with the bartender about him not getting another drink. This gu was loud and using profanity at the bartender. I could have left the bar, bu

I felt satisfied sitting where I was. After the argument was over, the bartender said to me that he was sorry that I had to hear that, so my meal was free. That meal was $40. I was at the right place at the right time, feeling satisfied with my decision of following my core by sitting there. In the religious world, we called this being blessed.

Another experience I had was buying a new car. My car was causing me some problems at the time. It had a lot of miles on the odometer, as it was over twenty years old. So, I started thinking about getting a new car. My credit was very bad and, on top of that, I had no money to put down on a new car. So, I figured that I'd wait until the following year to buy one, which, at the time, was nine months away. But my inner core drove me to start looking at the prices of new cars, since I hadn't made a payment on a car in over twenty years. I had no idea how much a car would cost. So, I began looking at the cost of cars on my computer. I put my phone number in to one of the dealerships and immediately received a call, inviting me to come down and see what they had to offer. Now, I curious about where my inner core was driving me to. I was obedient to its pulling and went to the dealership. While there, I made it very clear that I had no money, my old car had no value, and I wasn't prepared to purchase a car until the following year. And, on top of that, my credit was awful. I was simply there to see what vehicles cost. Yet, after about one hour, I drove off that lot with a new car and with monthly payments well below what I was expecting. Being led and obedient to my inner core, I received a fulfillment of satisfaction. I was at the right place at the right time. When you follow your gut or feelings of satisfaction, guided by the Word, which give you a moral center of direction, you'll always be at the right place at the right time. You'll be able to fulfill God's purpose for your life. People who live this way seem to be happier than others. Things seem to go their way all the time. Yes, they have some bad days, but it never seems to bother them because they speak of better times in their lives through prayer or conversations with family and friends. They seem to have figured out that whatever you put out there in the universe always comes back to you good or bad. It's like the boomerang effect, whatever you throw out comes back and affects your own life. We're designed to live for the Creator. Fish aren't swimming; they're being swum. Birds aren't flying; they're being flown. We aren't living; we're being lived.

We are made up of spiritual and physical matter. Our souls and spirits possess the power to overcome any obstacle or challenge the world has to offer; it's in our DNA, given to us by our Creator. We have the power to create and to destroy ourselves and our environment. When we choose to follow the inner pulling of our core spirit, based upon a religious foundation, we begin to live with a sense of satisfaction and confidence while fulfilling our purpose through serving others. We can laugh at obstacles and troubles that come our way because when a shift happens in us, all we see is joy as the result. We count it all joy because we live for God and we die for him. Within him, we have our life and well-being. We're able to fulfill the reason we came here to this world of confusion and chaos. The transformative power comes through our will. We are to become the transformative agent the world needs. Let our light so shine that everyone we come in contact with is affected by its brilliance. Let's use our religion as a foundation to live more spiritual as God designed us to be. We're here for only a very short time to complete our mission. So, ask yourself, "Have I done all I needed to do while in this life? Have I completed my work here on Earth? Is Source proud of me?" Never find yourself saying, "I wish I could have… I wish I should have… I wish I would have… Ask yourself, "While here on this Earth, have I helped someone along the way? Have I given of myself or practice random acts of kindness during my life here?" If you can answer yes to those questions, then you've lived a complete life and are ready for your transition back to where we all came from, Source.

What a spiritual journey I've been on! My faith and beliefs have been stretched and enlighten by the near-death experiencers I've interviewed. I've learned how to roll with the punches of life, fearing no evil because God's rod and staff comfort me. I've learned that all experiences don't last, but as you pass through them, you learn lessons. I've learned that worrying is no longer an option, knowing that if the Creator can take care of a bird that worries about nothing and eats every day, then I know he can take care of you. For you should know that you're more important to your Creator than a bird. I've learned to follow my inner core, sit still, and listen to the small voice in my gut that will lead me to all understanding. I've learned that there's a difference between faith and belief. I always thought that they were one in the same. I wasn't aware that I was following two words, "faith" and "belief," but couldn't explain how they worked together and being both different. Then I thought, *Wait a minute, they're two difference words, how can they mean the same?* Although most of the people in the church I went to believe the same, I struggled with that understanding.

I remember the Scripture saying that faith without works is dead. So, I looked up the two words and discovered that belief is something that you know, something that you have been taught, something that brings mental and emotional conviction through knowledge, but it does not necessarily produce results. This is what turns a lot of people off to the church. They see church folk talking about the importance of living a godly life but can't seem to be an example to it. Faith, however, is an action word. It's the active demonstration of what one believes or knows. This is why the scriptures says faith without works is dead. If you believe in something but are unable to act on that belief, it's just a belief. For example, you can believe that a glass of water will quench your thrust, but if you don't drink the water, which is the act of faith, you'll die of thirst, believing that the water will do that. Every person has an element of faith, even as tiny as a mustard seed. Getting up in the morning is an act of faith. Brushing your teeth is an act of faith, going to work is an act of faith, and mending broken relationships is an act of faith. Practicing forgiveness and repentance is an act of faith. The more you act, the more confident you are in doing. So, the only way to make your belief become a reality is to act on it. This is how we, as spiritual beings designed by God with all his power and ability, can create our reality. The most frustrating thing about religion is knowing what to do but not doing it. In other words, why do many of us struggle with the ability to live out what our religion tells us to do. I've learned that the more I act on my belief, the more confident I am in my faith. When you act on what you know, your faith becomes strong and no weapon can be used against you and you will prosper. You're unshaken by social challenges, political environment, and religions ideologies. So, it's very important to practice what you believe and not just go to your place of worship to just reinforce your belief. You know more than enough on how to live a moral and spiritual life; now, it's a choice.

One of the other things that I've discovered is the importance of having a lifestyle of meditation with its goal of turning off thoughts that ruminate in the vortex of my mind. This has helped me to avoid living in my past by focusing on past negative behaviors and failures. Although I still hold onto a lot of my old-school religion, ethics, and morals, resulting in my struggle with people who are of different transgender orientation, I do understand it and except it with no more judgment from my own religious point of view. My spirituality, to this day, is continuing to evolve. I no longer fear death, but look forward with tiptoe anticipation for my inevitable transition where I can see my long-lost relatives, particularly my sister. Although they're all around me and never left me but just in another dimension, connecting with them through meditations and prayer gives me hope. I don't want to commit suicide before my transition out of fear that once I'm in heaven, I'll be told that my work isn't done and I have to return. Once I'm there, I'm not coming back. Life is a one-shot deal for me, so I've got to get it right. I've got to fulfill my purpose.